HOME BUYING MADE EASY

SECRETS THAT WILL SAVE YOU THOUSANDS OF DOLLARS, HOURS OF TIME AND LOTS OF HEADACHES

Bill Desautels

ISBN-10: 148272751X
ISBN-13: 9781482727517

Library of Congress Control Number: 2013904808
CreateSpace Independent Publishing Platform
North Charleston, SC

I will never forget my first home, and you will never forget yours. So many people want to pursue the American dream, thinking their first homes are going to be their dream homes. Let me set the record straight: your first home may well be anything but a dream home. Instead, it may be something closer to a toad, warts and all. But you will fall in love with that wart-infested toad like it was Prince Charming.

When I was twenty-one (oh so many decades ago), my bride (oh so many lives ago) and I bought our first home together. To this day, it's still hard to describe exactly what I bought. Located in a quaint village in northern Vermont, from the outside, it looked like a picture-book Vermont farmhouse, complete with a barn out back. At some point during its 150-year history, it was converted to a duplex. Later, during the early phase of the condominium craze, it somehow morphed into an adjoining new construction project. Thus, I became the proud owner of a historic detached duplex condo.

To save money, we decided to live in the four-hundred-square-foot, one-bedroom unit with sloping floors and a virtually nonexistent kitchen. Thankfully, my bride's father was handy at renovations; so, in due time, it became livable. Meanwhile, we jumped into the landlord business—novices indeed. After placing some ads in our local paper, we finally settled in with our living companions.

At first all seemed fine; it was a bit noisy at times, but at least their rent paid much of our mortgage. We thought we had died and gone to heaven. Then one day, all seemed quiet downstairs. Days turned into weeks…no sign of the family of four. What really caught our attention was the raunchy smell of what can only be described as dead animals. If you haven't smelled it before, let me assure you, you will never forget it.

Reluctantly, with my father-in-law in tow, we ended up breaking into their apartment only to discover that rats were gnawing at the food left on the counters. There were even pork chops still in the oven. Our beautiful, quaint Vermont home had become some sort of refugee center. It wasn't until a few days later that we discovered what had happened to them: they were in jail on drug charges.

That began my saga of home ownership. So why would I tell you such a nasty tale of my first home? Because, despite the initial headache, to this day, I know that my decision to take the plunge into owning my own home was the right decision. It has not only led me to my dream home—now I am the proud owner of three homes. It all happened one step at a time. For you, moving from a rented home (or, worse yet, from living with your parents) to a place of your own will become one of the most empowering moments of your life.

So, join me along this path to a new chapter in your life. Within this book you will discover the tools and steps needed to get there. I will be sharing with you easy-to-follow, easy-to-replicate steps you can take to save yourself tens of thousands of dollars and countless nightmares.

TIME TO BUY?

So, is now the right time to buy? Hell, yes. That is, if you want the lowest prices and interest rates you are likely to see in your lifetime, which all leads to the greatest affordability in modern history. So you might be wondering, am I just another darned Realtor blowing smoke or perhaps smoking some weed? Actually, considering that I have been a real estate agent since the 1970s (at that time, I was eighteen and had a full set of braces), I have now experienced virtually every type of economic climate, from boom times to recessions—and damn, this last one was a doozie. I have guided over three thousand folks through the buying and selling process, many of whom I have had the pleasure of working with many times as they went from stepping stone to stepping stone, leading them to their dream homes.

I speak from experience—lots of it.

Although not all real estate markets are the same (some towns and cities do better than others), what I will be sharing will give you a snapshot that looks rather similar across the United States. I live in the tiny state of Vermont, where men wear plaids, women are fit, and, as Garrison Keeler would say, our children are above average.

  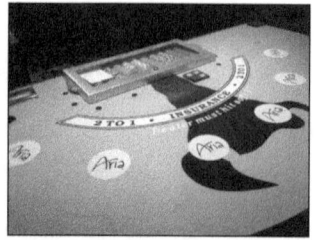

Here in Burlington, Vermont, our real estate market has faced some serious headwinds these past few years. Not nearly as bad as Florida or the city of sin, Las Vegas, but we have surely felt the impact of the financial meltdown. Our market has suffered through three major price corrections in the last thirty years.

1981	1989	2005
$66,807 peak price	$132,072 peak price	$343,361 peak price
Interest rate: 16.5%	Interest rate: 11%	Interest rate: 6.5%
No fixed rates	Fixed available	Fixed available
Time to buy?	Time to buy?	Time to buy?

It is now 2013. Prices of single-family homes are averaging $318,526; interest rates are around 3.875 percent. Although I do not have a crystal ball, if history is any indicator of the future, prices are ripe for rebounding. In fact, in my market, sales volume picked up last year by 18 percent, prices nudged up by a respectable 5.4 percent.

As you can see in the chart below, overall prices have continued to escalate; on average, they have gone up by about 3.3 percent per year.[1]

So, prices are ripe for taking off. What about interest rates—are they really that low? Not to bore you with charts, but buying a home is one of

---

[1] Data via MLS for Chittenden County, Vermont, 2012 sales statistics. Appreciation calculated based on price-per-square-foot comparisons.

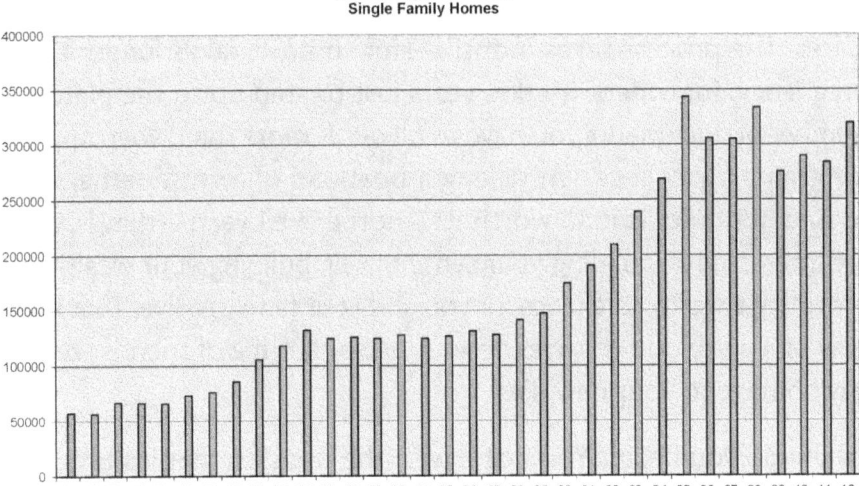

**Burlington
MLS Average Sales Price
Single Family Homes**

the biggest investments you will ever make. You probably ought to be taking more time to think about a wise move in your hunt for housing than you would to plan a trip to Mexico.

Let's talk about some finance options and why interest rates matter.

YOUR ROAD HOME

So you think you want to buy a home, really? It's important to keep in mind that it's not like running down to Macy's and buying a pair of sexy jeans, where you can actually try them on for size, check yourself out in the mirror, see how they make your hot derrière look...yeah, baby, I'm talking to you. Can you imagine people noticing you as you drift by, walking with incredible confidence, with your two-hundred dollar pair of designer jeans wrapped around your hips? You've got the picture. Hell yes, they are worth every penny. Swipe that credit card; I have a date tonight. Now, that was easy. Even with a bit of guilt after you get home, you are feeling mighty fine.

Buying a home, now, that's another matter. First off, you can't put it on your credit card unless, of course, you are Warren Buffet or Bill Gates. The process takes months—for some, it takes longer than a pregnancy; for others, it takes years just to step up to the plate. The number of documents you have to fill out is more than when applying for grants for college. I'm talking a boatload of forms, perhaps fifty to one hundred. Is it all worth it? Another hell yeah—that is, if you are interested in building your sense of self, building your wealth, and providing a warm, safe place for you and your family to live. That family may be your blood relatives or your personal tribe of friends who will pay homage to your new digs.

Where do you begin? You begin with the decision that it's time for a new chapter in your life; it's time you stop living with your parents, and it's time to stop renting flea-infested apartments. It's time to be your own landlord for a change, one who actually cares about whether your heat functions properly, whether the paint is peeling, and who cares about who you are as a person. That landlord is you. When you own a home, you are in the driver's seat of your future. You alone are laying the course for your future. Don't get me wrong, many people are doing just fine, living with Mom and Dad or sharing a flat with a roommate. If "just fine" is what you are after, keep on renting and staying with family. Think about some of your role models. Think about some of the most successful people you know—the owners of your favorite businesses, both locally and on the world stage. Do they rent or live with Mom and Dad? No, they don't, and they have something in common with where you are at today—they all bought their first home.

Now, let's look at an overview of the process ahead. This roadmap has many turns, some sharp, some gentler; on occasion, you may be forced back to the starting line. As long as you know your ultimate outcome, you will find your way; you will land on the bright red X called "home."

Initial Interview with Realtor

Meet with a Lender and Obtain a Pre-Approval

See Property (Bring Your Checkbook)

Make an Offer

Negotiate

Offer Accepted

Contract (Not Official Without **ALL** Signatures)

- Meet with Lender to Formalize Application

- Choose an Attorney

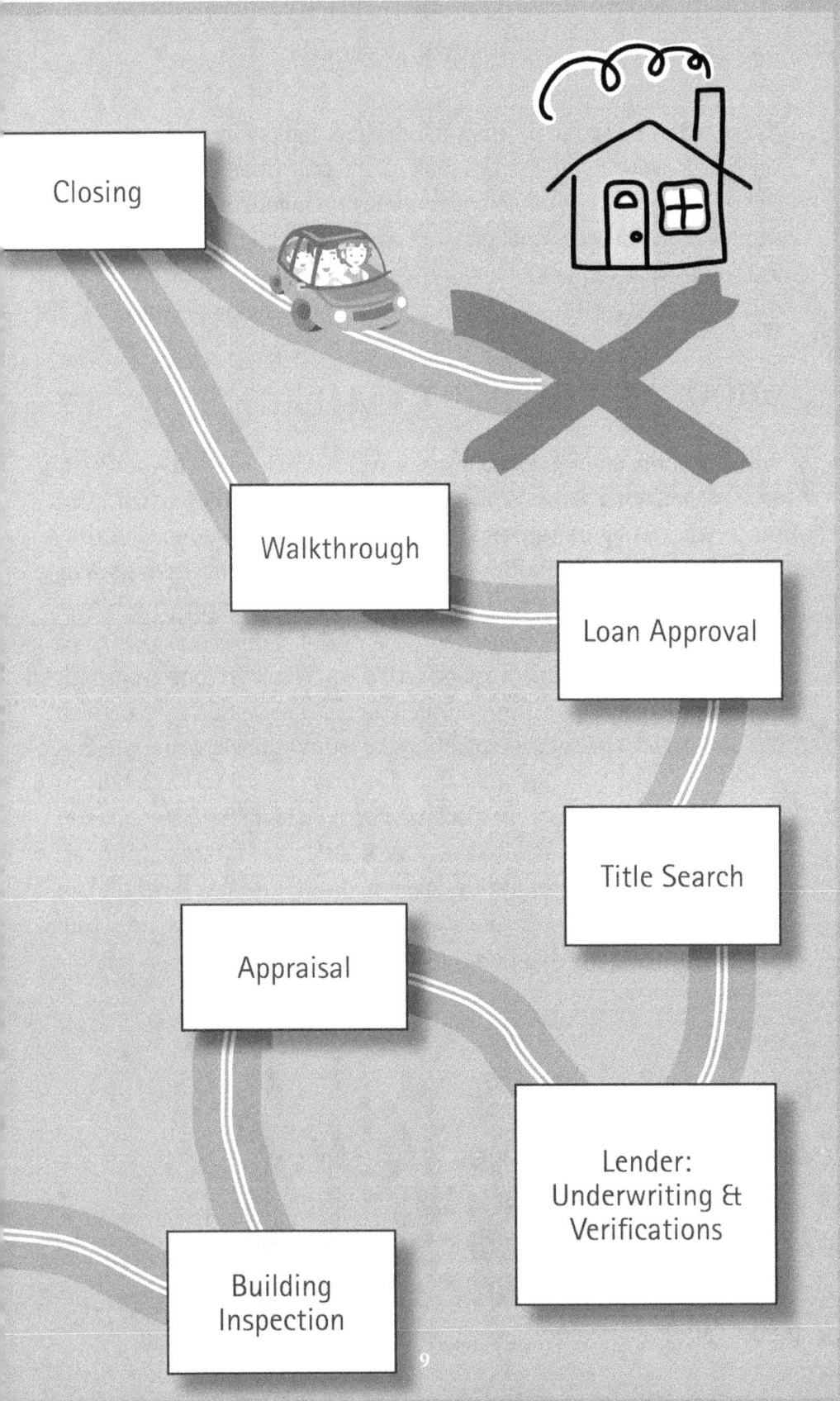

Closing

Walkthrough

Loan Approval

Title Search

Appraisal

Lender:
Underwriting &
Verifications

Building
Inspection

As you can see, the road looks daunting; it looks like a lot to handle. Let me ask you, if you need to make a 250-mile drive, how do you get there? The short and obvious answer is one mile at a time. There are dozens of turns, occasional pit stops, some refueling, and putting your foot on the gas required. Now is the time to put your foot on the gas, driving toward a more empowering future of home ownership.

CHOOSING THE RIGHT TEAM

Buying a home requires lots of players; you are likely to need a great real estate agent, not a Vanna White who tells you, "Here is the kitchen." That much you can figure out on your own; you need someone who truly cares about you. Your Realtor has to understand your needs in housing, but more importantly, he or she needs to understand your wants. A Realtor who is worth every penny he or she earns is one who has a serious amount of experience. God forbid you or a loved one ever needs open heart surgery, but if you do, are you going to want a surgeon who has performed a few dozen operations, or would you want one who has done hundreds? You also want that doctor to regard you as a human being and not just as another success, a notch on his or her belt; you want a person who truly cares. Likewise, your Realtor needs to have your best interests in mind and not just be concerned with how fast he or she can get more money. You need a Realtor who knows how to negotiate in your best interest, one who has been down this road before.

How do you pick the right Realtor for you? Great question—but perhaps the real question is how to avoid Realtors who mainly worry about their bottom line and couldn't care less about you making a choice that supports who *you* are. Turning to friends can be helpful; I actually think one trusted adviser helps lead to the rest. Start by asking a friend whom they would recommend as an attorney, and then ask them whom they would use if that person weren't available. So now you have two attorneys you can call to discover whom you should hire as your real estate agent. Let each attorney know that you are a first-time homebuyer and what type of home you are searching for, and then ask that attorney to name three agents who would take good care of you. After running that same question by both attorneys, one agent is likely to be mentioned more than once. There's a good chance you can count on that Realtor to work in your best interest and actually give a damn about how you are treated in the process.

But if that doesn't feel comfortable for you, here are some questions to ask the agent you are thinking about hiring:

1) How long have you been in the business? *Look for someone with a minimum of five years—ideally someone who has experienced a variety of real estate markets including boom times and bust times, allowing them to give you a sense of likely real estate trends ahead.*

2) How many homes have you sold thus far? *Anything less than one hundred probably isn't enough; although he or she might have great enthusiasm, you need more than a cheerleader—you need an advocate on your side, a fighter who knows when to push and when to pull back.*

3) What areas do you serve, regarding both physical locations and types of real estate? *If the person is willing to drive much farther than seems normal, or if he or she claims to be able to handle all kinds of real estate, from condos to commercial, run, don't walk. This is not the time for a jack-of-all-trades. Realtors need*

to work within a reasonable geographic area as well as a specific housing type, rather than justifying covering the entire state and handling sales from condos to commercial properties. Anything less than that may mean the agent is focused on themselves and not the outcome for you.

4) Do you have a team? If so, what does it consist of? *Imagine going to see that doctor for open heart surgery; do you really want him or her to photocopy your insurance card, weigh you in, take your blood pressure, do the actual lab reports, handle the billing, and sterilize the surgical equipment? No, you want the doctor to do what he or she does best and leave the rest to others on the team.*

5) What systems will you be using to discover *the* right home? *Does the Realtor like to work with for-sale-by-owners? Does he or she contact other agents to let them know he or she has a qualified buyer ready to go? Does he or she do mailings to target neighborhoods, when inventory is too low?*

6) Am I allowed to terminate our buyer broker agreement at any time, without penalty, if I am not satisfied with your services? *I believe if the agent is as good as he or she claims, he or she will have no problem allowing you to move on and hire someone different, someone more in tune with your needs and wants.*

MEANWHILE, GET YOUR FINANCIAL HOUSE IN ORDER: *KNOW THY CREDIT SCORE!*

When is the last time you saw your credit score? Perhaps you have been too scared to even peek at the numbers. That is probably a good reason why you must do exactly that, before you get too deep into the lending process. FICO[2] and other credit rating companies can directly affect your

---

[2] FICO is a public company that provides credit scoring to help lenders make decisions.

mortgage rates. Paying literally tens of thousands more, just because you missed the cutoff by a mere three or four points, makes absolutely no sense at all. I have found that buyers are receiving very little advice on how to improve their credit scores. Much of the advice given can actually cause more harm than good, so navigate this minefield carefully.

Many real estate offices can run credit reports *free* of charge. This will help give you a sense of your financial capabilities. A good Realtor will know how to help you read the problem areas and guide you in correcting the obvious. At the very least, the agent will be able to direct you to trusted names of credit counselors. Not the late-night infomercial folks who sell you nothing more than snake oils. I'm once again talking about people who care about your outcome and not just receiving your hard-earned cash. So how much can you expect to pay? In the ballpark of three hundred to five hundred dollars for them to negotiate with your creditors to improve items on your credit report and thereby improve your credit score. I know, I know, that is a lot of money, but you will save that amount tenfold over time. OK, you don't have the extra money, I get it. In that case, here are some quick tips to improve your credit score:

1) Look for the obvious. Sometimes items show up that you never even borrowed for; sometimes they literally have the wrong guy. Medical companies are notorious for not letting lenders know a prior delinquent bill has been brought into good standing.

2) Pay down credit lines as much as you can for two to three months; be aggressive! Build that financial muscle.

3) Do *not* close unused accounts; that can actually work against you. It makes you appear to be backing yourself into a corner, with no place to turn for purchases.

4) If you still feel inclined to melt your credit cards, hold on to the oldies with history, and kiss the newborns good-bye (I'm talking credit cards, folks—lighten up!).

5) Move the balances around, so your cards have a more even distribution, rather than having one or two credit cards near or at their limits.

These credit reporting companies offer services to run you through a variety of options—hopefully, options that won't tie you in knots. Consider visiting *myFICO.com* for some ways to tweak your credit score.

As for the bankers, lenders, mortgage officers—they are called many different things—think of them as the gal with the cash you need, lots of cash.

FINANCING

My dad passed away over twenty years ago, but this simple man had some wonderful lessons to share. He was an avid gardener, and God, his tomatoes were plump, tasty, and juicy. He knew that he had to keep the garden free of weeds; otherwise, the vegetables he was trying to grow wouldn't have a fighting chance. Well, the same holds true in growing your wealth. I know. You are simply trying to find a home to call your own, a place where you and your cat or dog (or child) can curl up on the  couch, watch some TV, and drift off to sleep. Providing a home is most important, but your home is also a large investment; done wisely it will lead to a road of riches.

The following info blew me away when I first stumbled onto this research. Each day, you toil at work, earning one dollar at a time, much of which will pay for taxes to the government. Of what is left over, the biggest expense, by far, is housing. As a renter, you are indeed paying off a mortgage—your landlord's mortgage. Your landlord is the one building his or her wealth and net worth. Did you know that according to a 2007 Federal Reserve study, the average net worth of a homeowner was $200,000, whereas the net worth of a renter was a mere $5,000?

Let's face it: Americans are notoriously bad at saving money, so owning a home is a great way to have forced savings. By that, with each and every mortgage payment you make, much of it is applied to your principal balance. When it comes time to sell, you'll walk away with a bigger check.

So, let's look at some financing options. To this day, in most areas of the country, you can still buy with *nothing down*, and there are many options of getting involved in home ownership with 3–5 percent down. The programs are too vast to discuss here; your lender will provide you with guidance as to what programs are available in your state.

What I want to talk about are some choices you can make when it comes to acquiring a loan on a home. At first glance, rate may seem like the only thing to be considering; however, the flexibility of your lender may matter more.

Monthly vs. Biweekly Mortgage Payments

Based on a $250,000 loan with 3.875% interest. Standard monthly payments would be $1,175.59 or biweekly payments would be $587.80.

	Standard	Biweekly
Loan Length	30 years	26 years
Monthly Payment	$1,175.59	$1273.56
Total Interest Paid (over the life of the loan)	$173,213.38	$146,930.08

Total benefit with adjusted tax savings is **$19,449.64**.

15-, 20-, or 30-Year Loan

The chart below shows what the cost is monthly (principal and interest) based on a 15-, 20-, or 30-year mortgage of $250,000 for various interest rates.

Interest Rate	15 Year Loan	20 Year Loan	30 Year Loan
3.50%	$1,787.21	$1,449.90	$1,122.61
3.75%	$1,818.06	$1,482.22	$1,157.79
4.00%	$1,849.22	$1,514.95	$1,193.54
4.25%	$1,880.70	$1,548.09	$1,229.85
4.50%	$1,912.48	$1,581.62	$1,266.71
4.75%	$1,944.58	$1,615.56	$1,304.12
5.00%	$1,976.98	$1,649.89	$1,342.05

I know none of us wants to have to live on peanut butter and jelly sandwiches for the rest of our lives, but you will be surprised at how easy it is to pay a bit more each month. Come on, find your muscles; you are stronger than you think. What you decide today will shape your tomorrows for years to come.

So how do you find a good lender? Assuming you trust the judgment of your friends—not all friends make the best choices—I think their recommendations are a great place to start. I have found that, although Internet-based mortgage companies might offer attractive rates, they tend to make the process far more cumbersome than it needs to be. Perhaps because I'm in my fifties, I'm somewhat old-fashioned, and I still like putting a face to the person handling my important things in life, be it my doctor or my banker. Assuming you have a credit union in your area, it can be a great source for first-time buyers and tend to offer a wide range of options.

The array of financing options is vast; it looks like the land of alphabet soup out there. FHA, VA, RD, ARM[3] are just some of the options you

---

[3] See glossary at the end of this book for explanations of these terms.

can turn to. Most states have a first-time homeowners program; here in Vermont, it is called the Vermont Housing Finance Agency (VHFA). Their goal is to make it easier to buy your first home, most often with excellent rates, lower closing costs, and, perhaps more importantly, much lower down payment requirements.

SWEAT EQUITY FINANCING OPTIONS

Throughout the United States, most states have a variety of programs that make affordability a reality. They are referred to as land trusts. Here in Vermont, we are home to perhaps the nation's most successful land trust, Champlain Housing Land Trust (formerly known as Burlington Community Land Trust). So, how does a land trust work? Well, in a nutshell, they tend to give interest-free or ultra-low grants to buyers; in return, when you sell the home, you do not receive the full appreciation. You still get to enjoy all of the benefits of home owner-ship, including the freedom to be creative with your personal touches, and you also get the tax benefits available to homeowners. I have had the privilege of working with many land trusts and have spoken at their national conferences. Clearly, not everyone will gravitate to using the land trust option; however, it is an amazing tool to consider as a stepping stone toward your future.

I'M FEELING NEEDY AND WANT SO MUCH MORE

So you are about to meet with your Realtor of choice in a few hours; now what? You and your significant other have two darling children (at least, you think so). Max, the rambunctious one, is tall for an eight-year-old, and Ariana is such a princess for a three-year-old. They both are a tad demanding, not unusual for kids these days; they don't know when to stop asking for more. How many times have you told them money doesn't grow on trees? Apparently not often enough, because they are insisting on separate bedrooms.

Max actually thinks he can't live without a private bath (perhaps I have the princess thing wrong).

This is where *needs* meet *wants*. I grew up in a large household; I am the youngest of eight kids. We lived in a tougher part of town, growing up poor—not dirt poor, but damned close. I will never forget our family cars over the years; just getting them started was quite the  experience. One dusty pink car had to be pushed down our street a couple of blocks as we made our way to Depot Street. Depot Street was a steep road that ended at the railroad tracks. As we huffed and puffed, my dad would jump into the driver's seat as the kids would pile into the backseat; somehow, as we gained momentum down the hill, my dad managed to get the gears engaged, and behold, we were on our way. Thankfully, not all days were like this; sometimes it would start like normal cars: key in the ignition, foot on the clutch, and presto. It got us to where we needed to go, which was never far, but just far enough.

Our home had absolutely everything we could possibly need: a kitchen, bedrooms, and a bath. Yes, the ten of us shared a bath, and trust me, we had a way of letting each other know when it was time to clear a path. I mean really clear a path! As for the bedrooms, my parents had one, and the eight of us shared the other two. My bed consisted of a crib for way too many years; I blame my height (or lack thereof) on my restricted space for growth.

I understand that there are times when needs blur with wants; they can be a little of both. Heck, if I had eight kids, which I don't, there is no way I would want to live in a home with one bath. No way. When you meet with your Realtor, be sure to be crystal clear on what your true needs are. Keep in mind that the needs aren't the items that will cost you; it's your wants that are most expensive. The view of the lake, you can live without; you want a room to accommodate a pool table; you want a home in the "Hill Section"; that's all fine. But keep in mind that they are going to cost you; some of them will cost you big time.

There's nothing wrong with wanting; in fact, my belief is that wants are the motivation behind most large purchases. Think about the last three or four items you bought that you normally wouldn't splurge on; whether a whimsical watch or an extravagant dining experience, you could have lived without them. But you wanted it so badly, so you managed to justify it to yourself—and perhaps even to your partner. Live it, breathe it, own it, and acknowledge what we all know: you sure as heck didn't need it. Want is a powerful force, be it for a watch or a home.

During your initial interview with your Realtor, make sure you are open with your needs versus wants. And make sure that you are shopping within your financial restraints; you might just find you can live without some items, but there are at least one or two items that cannot be compromised. What are they?

Needs:

_____ _____
_____ _____
_____ _____
_____ _____
_____ _____

Wants:

_____ _____
_____ _____
_____ _____
_____ _____
_____ _____

SHOPPING TIME

Depending on where you live, you likely have hundreds—perhaps thousands—of homes for sale within just a few miles from where you live now. Ninety percent of them can be eliminated right off the bat because of price, condition, or because they don't come close to meeting your needs. A good agent should be able to whittle this number down to a half dozen or so, provided the two of you have dug deep into what you are searching for. As a member of a multiple listing service (MLS), your agent can show you homes listed with his or her firm—or with any real estate firm across town, for that matter. Heck, your Realtor can even assist you in pursuing a home being marketed directly as a for-sale-by-owner. Indeed, in most areas, a high percentage of for-sale-by-owners are actually sold by Realtors. *One of the most important things a respected buyer's agent does for you is make sure you are not paying too much for a home, especially from an unrepresented seller.*

Often I am asked how many homes a buyer needs to see before he or she should be ready to make an offer. My answer is one—yes, just one. For if you and your Realtor both have drilled down on your needs and wants, and you have reviewed many of the possibilities online, with dozens of photos, virtual tours, and videos, it can be weeded down to just one.

Beginning to seem a bit real, isn't it? You may want to bring your checkbook along, just in case your agent *is* that good.

As for how long you should spend in each home, for most people, it comes down to five to ten minutes, unless of course this home feels like "the one", by all means spend as much time as you need. On your first time out, the agent may not tune into your standards, and you might stumble into a dump. In that case, if you absolutely know you could not live there, do a 180, exit the building like it's on fire, and hope you discover something a bit more promising on your next stop. If your agent doesn't ask probing questions while touring, spill your guts and tell him or her how you feel. Is the kitchen just way too small for your culinary skills, or does the yard offer privacy you said you couldn't live without?

After seeing a few homes, eliminate the ones that don't even meet your basic needs. I like using the 1–10 scale; on the top of each data sheet, write down your rating of each home. If it's a 7 or higher, it's worth considering making an offer. Keep in mind that you will not find a home that meets 100 percent of your needs and wants, so you should be shooting for 85 percent. Even the Taj Mahal has its flaws; it has way too many tiles, and it's in the middle of a dusty desert.

LET'S MAKE A DEAL

At some point, you will find *the* home. You know what I mean—you've just *got* to have it. Get your ass back to the real estate office and get started with the paperwork; it's time to put ink to paper, baby. The problem is that you are clueless as to how much the place is really worth, and you certainly don't want to overpay, so now what? First, get your emotions under control; otherwise, you will become irrational during the negotiations. Some folks may be willing to pay too much; for others, you allow a measly five dollars per month get in the way of you finally getting a home. Finally, you can move out of your parents' home.

Keeping in mind your financial cap, you now have to decide if the asking price is fair or not. Is the seller smoking weed and in la-la land, or is this place a hot item that will be sold quickly if you don't act? Too many people think that all properties are going to sit around forever, just waiting for them to decide what they are going to do. No matter how tough the economy is, many properties are priced so well or are so unique that multiple bids will come in the day they hit the market. If you trust your real estate agent, take his or her advice. Of course, ask for backup information. Just like when a seller hires an agent to help establish a listing price, you can also have the agent do what's called a CMA (comparable market analysis). It will compare the home you

Sold Date		8/31/12		
DOM		4		
Taxes		4331		
Town	Williston	Williston		
Year Built	1999	1998		
Gross Liv Area	1604 AG	2192 AG	-$29,400	
Water Frontage	None			
Style	Townhouse	End Unit		
Exterior	Clapboard	Clapboard		
Construction	Existing	Existing		
Bedrooms	2	3	-$4,000	
Full Baths	2	2	$0	
Half Baths	1	1	$0	
3/4 Baths	0	0	$0	
# Rooms	5	5	$0	
Heat/Cool	Forced Air	Baseboard		
Fuel	Gas-Natural	Gas-Natural		
Garage	Attached	Attached		
# Cars	1	1	$0	
Driveway	Paved	Paved		
Basement	Full, unfinished	Crawl Space		
Int. Features		1st Floor Laundry		
Int. Features		1st Floor Master		
Ext. Features	Deck	Deck		
Lot Desc.		Country Setting		

hope to own to others in the neighborhood. After adjusting for square footage, number of bedrooms, baths, acreage, and the like, you will be given a range of likely sale prices. Make sure the agent pulls data from the MLS and also from public records whenever possible. Keep in mind that these days, you do have a bit of a safety net when it comes to not overpaying for a home. During the financing stage, the lender will hire an appraiser to make sure both the lender and their investors are well protected when it comes to value. That is one minor silver lining to the financial meltdown of 2008; no one wants to go over that cliff again.

Earlier I mentioned five dollars per month. What I'm getting at is the cost per thousand dollars of the money you will be borrowing for your home. The chart below indicates the actual cost per thousand, based on a loan of thirty years (amortization) at various interest rates.

My question for you is, do you want the home badly enough to spend an extra five, ten, or twenty dollars a month to get it? If not, stick firmly to your offer and be willing to move on without regrets.

Cost per Thousand Financed

Interest Rate	Monthly Cost per Thousand
3.50%	$4.49
3.75%	$4.63
4.00%	$4.77
4.25%	$4.92
4.50%	$5.07
4.75%	$5.22
5.00%	$5.37

Now, back to the offer writing. This is serious stuff; that's why you will be signing about a dozen documents just to place an offer on the home. Do not take this lightly. If the seller agrees to it, you are legally bound; yes, there are paragraphs that allow you a legal out, but be careful not to miss any of the critical dates set forth. In most states, after you have written an offer, it will be submitted to the other real estate agent and the seller for the start of negotiations. The options for the seller are rather straightforward: they can reject it outright, accept it as written, or (most likely) counter your original offer. Counters are usually done verbally, and they are rarely enforceable. What do I mean by that? I mean that even if the seller has verbally committed to sell the home to you, if every single change isn't initialed by both sides, another offer could come in from an even more excited buyer, and the seller might choose to accept the new buyer's offer. Yes, it's maddening and can seem unfair, but in most states, it is totally legal.

Over the years I have often found both buyers and sellers who get involved with negotiations and they "play not to lose" rather than "play to win." Knowing your desired outcome is critical to any negotiation; too many buyers get so hung up on not paying too much that they lose out on a great home and a property that will be a good investment over time. Perhaps it is a thousand dollars or so higher than the most recent sale, it's also possible that soon after you purchase your home, the next sale might be a thousand dollars higher still. Stop looking for obstacles; instead, look for the magic.

NUTS AND BOLTS OF THE PURCHASE & SALE CONTRACT

When it's time to make an offer it is done on a Purchase and Sale Contract; they vary a bit state by state, but much of the language is similar. A contact is not to be taken lightly; it is a legally binding agreement between you and the seller. Pay attention to all the paragraphs, it's not just about price and closing date; the Devil is in the details.

I want to spell out in layman's terms what each paragraph means. I will avoid legal jargon and by all means never hesitate to turn to legal counsel to learn the potential ramifications of each and every sentence. Normally the standard Purchase and Sale Contracts aren't reviewed by an attorney prior to signing, but if unusual language is added it's not a bad idea to add language such as "subject to satisfactory review by purchaser's attorney within two business days."

So let's start from the top. I will put in each paragraph word for word followed by my interpretation and some shared stores of things that have occurred over the years. The contract I am showing for demonstration purposes is copywrited by the Vermont Association of Realtors and may not be used without their written permission.

Prior to getting into the paragraphs, the players are identified. It's critical that full legal names and addresses are available; this becomes particularly important when one party wishes to terminate due to one contingency or another.

1.   **Purchase and Sale Contract:** This Purchase and Sale Contract (Contract) is made by and between _____ _____ (Seller) and _____ _____ (Purchaser). Purchaser agrees to purchase and Seller agrees to sell the Property described herein at the price and on the terms and conditions stated in this Contract.

A bit redundant, but it spells out the obvious, the buyer wants to buy and the seller wants to sell a certain property.

2.   **Total Purchase Price:** _____ _____ U.S. Dollars ($_____)

The amount you are offering is written out in longhand and numerically, naturally it refers to US dollars.

3.   **Contract Deposit:** $ _____ (US Dollars) as evidenced by □ **Personal check** □ **Bank check** □ **Cash** □ **Wire transfer**
Additional Contract Deposit of $_____ (US Dollars) is due within _____ calendar days after Seller's acceptance of offer.

Unless otherwise agreed in writing, the pendency of any contingencies or special conditions in this Contract does not suspend or postpone Purchaser's obligation to make any required additional Contract Deposit. All Contract Deposit(s) shall be held by: _____ _____ ("Escrow Agent"). If Purchaser's offer is not accepted, expires or is withdrawn prior to Seller's acceptance, all Contract Deposit(s) shall be promptly returned to Purchaser.

Here is where you identify the amount of the deposit, often the deposit amount comes in two stages. Some at the initial offer and

quite frequently more is required after acceptance and sometimes after the satisfactory building inspection. Deposits are made payable to
either the agency representing the seller or perhaps an attorney. These
funds are held in a trust account, more on potential disputes of the
deposit later. As noted in the event negotiations are not successful the
deposit is promptly returned in full.

4.   **Description of Real Property:** For purposes of this Contract,
      the Property is described as follows:

      A. Property Address: _____

      _____
      _____; and/or

      B. Seller's Deed recorded in Volume _____at Page(s)
      _____of the _____ Land
      Records; and/or

      C. Parcel ID number: _____
      _____; and/or

      D. SPAN Number: _____
      _____

      E. The Property is further described as: _____
      _____
      _____
      _____

      NOTE: *Not every Property Description choice is required in
      order to form this Contract. The validity and enforceability of
      this Contract is not affected by the omission of one or more of
      the above choices, provided at least one choice is filled in. The*
      deed delivered by Seller at Closing will govern the legal descrip-
      tion of the real property to be conveyed under this Contract.

Of course you want to identify the actual property you wish to buy, while only one description is needed, not a bad idea to be ultra-clear and identify it in more than one way.

True story, I once showed up at a closing on April Fool's Day. Keep in mind, the seller had evicted his tenant in anticipation of the scheduled closing, drove to Vermont in a snowstorm and fully expected to close. When I arrived the real estate agent that "sold" the condo said we weren't closing. Just prior to the closing the buyer and his Realtor went back to the condo to do the final walkthrough, when they arrived they saw a cat in the window. They knocked on the door, and the person inside was clueless as to what they were talking about. As it turns out, the Realtor had accidently shown the wrong property, the buyer looked at an end unit which happened to be unlocked (you will have that in Vermont). They wrote up the offer on my condo listing, put in the correct address, and of course the appraiser went to my condo listing, the bank approved the loan and we were all set. The thing was, the buyer only wanted an end unit.

Long story short, the Realtor made good on his error and bought the condo I had listed, what a surprise to his wife.

5.   **Closing:** Closing and transfer of title shall occur on the _____ day of _____, 20_____ at a mutually agreed time and place. Closing may occur earlier if Seller and Purchaser agree in writing. **Neither party shall be obligated to extend the date set for Closing.**

This is the critical closing date, the date you would expect to be fully ready to pay the purchase price and right after you should be able to move in. Over the past few years these dates are a moving target with new underwriting rules coming into play every day. Also, if you are buying a condo most likely the Vermont Division of Fire Safety will need to do an inspection and they are known to be working on overload. This date is meant to be taken seriously, if it looks like you will have a delay better to address ASAP so the proper extensions can be drafted, keep in mind the seller is not obligated to extend.

6. **Financing Contingency:** Purchaser's obligation to close under this Contract □ is □ is **not** subject to a financing contingency that Purchaser obtain mortgage financing in the amount of _____% of the purchase price for a term of _____ years at an interest rate not higher than _____% fixed for the term of the loan or _____% variable on the date of closing with not more than _____ points to be paid at Closing. Purchaser agrees to act diligently to obtain such financing and shall, **within _____ calendar days after this Contract is executed by Seller and Purchaser and notice thereof is provided to Purchaser in the manner required by Section 29**, submit a complete and accurate application for first mortgage financing to at least one mortgage lender or mortgage broker currently providing or placing such loans requesting first mortgage financing **in the amount and on the terms set forth above.** If Purchaser fails to timely submit such an application, this financing contingency is **waived** by Purchaser.

If, despite best efforts, Purchaser is unable to obtain a written commitment from a mortgage lender for the financing set forth above on terms satisfactory to Purchaser by _____ _____, 20___, Purchaser (but not Seller) shall have the right to TERMINATE this Contract provided Purchaser gives written notice to Seller of the inability to obtain such financing within four (4) calendar days after the above date in the manner required by Section 29. If Purchaser fails to do so, Purchaser's right to terminate this Contract on account of the Financing Contingency is waived. In the event Purchaser terminates this Contract in accordance with the provisions of this Section, all Contract Deposit(s), shall be forthwith returned to Purchaser, the Contract shall be terminated and shall be of no further force and effect. In such case, Seller and Purchaser agree to execute and deliver to Escrow Agent an authorization for delivery of all Contract Deposit(s) to Purchaser. If Purchaser's obligation to close **IS** subject to a financing contingency, Purchaser provides the following information:

a) Purchaser ☐ has ☐ has not consulted with a mortgage lender or mortgage broker about mortgage financing as of the date of Purchaser's offer.

b) Purchaser has obtained a mortgage lender's pre-approval or pre-qualification letter. ☐ Yes ☐ No. If Purchaser's obligation to close **IS NOT** subject to a financing contingency, Purchaser represents to Seller that Purchaser has sufficient cash or liquid assets to close on the purchase of the Property

This one's a doozy and it's the longest one found in the P&S. You need to let the seller know how you intend to pay for the home. While about 25% of the sales are in cash, the majority require financing. It is rare that a buyer would get this far without having met with a lender to determine qualifications. That being said, the specific loan terms are placed here with the amount you plan to put down, the type of loan (fixed or variable) together with when you expect the lender to have financing all approved. While there is a line for interest rates it is more common to see the words "prevailing" to indicate that should the rates creep up a bit you do not have the right to terminate due to that. There are some critical deadlines on financing, be careful not to miss them or your deposit could be in jeopardy. Provided proper notice is given and you have proof of being turned down for the loan, you would be entitled to your deposit back. Keep in mind many real estate offices will not release a deposit until such time both the buyer and seller have signed a mutual release.

Do you remember the shock of when OJ Simpson was acquitted? There are always two sides to every tale, and thus we cannot assume the obvious outcome.

7. **Lead-Based Paint:** Based upon representations made by Seller and Purchaser's own investigation and information, it is agreed that the Property ☐ **is** ☐ **is not** pre-1978 residential real estate and therefore ☐ **is** ☐ **is not** subject to Federal (EPA/HUD), State and, if applicable, Municipal

Lead-Based Paint Regulations. If the Property is pre-1978 residential real estate, the parties must execute a Lead-Based Paint Addendum with required disclosures, which shall become part of this Contract. Lead-Based Paint Addendum and Disclosures attached ☐ **Yes** ☐ **No**

State and Federal laws mandate that the seller disclose whether the home falls within the timeframe of when lead paint may have been used. If the home is believed to have been built pre-1978 an additional document will be attached in what is called an Addendum.

8. **Property Inspection Contingency.** Purchaser's obligation to close under this Contract ☐ **is** ☐ **is not** subject to a property inspection contingency. If this Contract is subject to a property inspection contingency, the parties must execute a **Property Inspection Contingency Addendum** which shall become part of this Contract.

While home inspections are not mandated, they are a good idea especially if you are buying an older home. Still to this date, many states do not have licensing standards for inspectors. Indeed, here in Vermont if I wanted to become an inspector I could be one within 24 hours. That being said, I have a great deal of respect for the job performed by our inspectors. An addendum will be attached if you choose to have an inspection done.

9. **General Addendum to Contract:** A General Addendum containing additional terms signed by Seller and Purchaser is attached hereto and made a part of this contract. ☐ **Yes** ☐ **No.**

Now this is a catch-all for things such as personal property, the appraisal contingency, receipt of sellers property information report, amongst others.

10. **Special Conditions:** _____

_____

_____

_____

This one can get messy, and if it feels like it's loosely written by all means run it by your attorney. Anything from how many dogs you can have at the condo, to finalizing a divorce can be found here. Often if the property is tenant occupied special provisions will be addressed here as well.

11. **Condominium/Common Interest Community.**   If the Property is a condominium unit, part of a common interest community, planned community, planned unit development (PUD) or other property subject to the Vermont Common Interest Ownership Act, a Common Interest Ownership Addendum is required.   Common Interest Ownership Addendum attached. ☐ **Yes**   ☐ **No**

If you are buying either a condo or certain single family homes that pay some type of association fees, yet another addendum needs to be added.

12. **State and Local Permits:** The parties acknowledge that certain state and local permits may govern the use of the Property. To the best of the Seller's knowledge, the Property is in compliance with any existing permits. Further, Seller has not received notice of violation(s) of any State or Local permit that has not been cured or resolved, unless otherwise disclosed in writing.

When a homeowner makes improvements, unless just cosmetic, a building permit may have been required. When your attorney does a title search they will check on both local and state permits making sure the home is in compliance. If not, this could definitely cause a delay in closing. Perhaps I overstated the Easy part in the title of this book, taken collectively this all goes rather smoothly for most purchases.

13. _**Limitation of Liability:** Seller and Purchaser each agree that the real estate brokers identified in Section 31 hereof have provided_

both Seller and Purchaser with benefits, services, assistance and value in bringing about this Contract. In consideration thereof, and in recognition of the relative risks, rewards, compensation and benefits arising from this transaction to said real estate brokers, **Seller and Purchaser each agree that such brokers, their agents, associates or affiliates, shall in no event be liable to either Purchaser, Seller or both, either jointly, severally or individually, in an aggregate amount exceeding the total compensation to be paid to such brokers on account of this transaction or $5,000, whichever is greater, by reason of any act or omission, including negligence, misrepresentation, errors and omissions, or breach of any undertaking whatsoever, except for intentional or willful acts.** *This limitation shall apply regardless of the cause of action or legal theory asserted against the real estate brokers unless the claim is for an intentional or willful act. This limitation of liability shall apply to all claims, losses, costs, damages or claimed expenses of any nature whatsoever from any cause or causes, except intentional or willful acts, so that the total aggregate liability of all real estate brokers identified in Section 31 hereof shall not exceed the amount set forth herein. Seller and Purchaser each agree that there is valid and sufficient consideration for this limitation of liability and that the real estate brokers are the intended third-party beneficiaries of this provision.*

The best way to describe this is to simply say this is to cover the Realtor's hide. While I have never been sued in my 3,000 sales, the potential litigation is huge. This paragraph caps how much an agent can be sued for.

14. **Possession:** Possession and occupancy of the premises, together with all keys/access devices or codes to the premises and any property or fixtures that are part of the sale, shall be given to Purchaser at Closing unless otherwise agreed in writing. Seller shall leave the premises broom clean, free from all occupants, and shall remove all personal property not being sold here-

under, together with the personal property of all occupants. Seller agrees to permit Purchaser to inspect the premises within 24 hours prior to the date set for Closing to insure compliance with this provision.

In theory, the seller must vacate the home at least 24 hours prior to closing so you can verify all possessions are gone as well as the seller. I must say, this rarely goes off like clockwork; indeed it is more common that the seller is still moving out or cleaning up just a few hours prior to closing. If, God forbid, the seller hasn't moved out in a timely manner, there is a decent chance your attorney may need to step in to correct the problem.

15.   **Payment of Purchase Price:** Payment of the purchase price is due at Closing and shall be adjusted for any Contract Deposit(s) held by Escrow Agent to be disbursed at closing, taxes or tax withholding applicable to Seller as described in Sections 17 and 18 of this Agreement, or as required by other applicable law, Closing Adjustments under Section 26 of this Agreement, compensation due to Seller's real estate broker, and any other items agreed to in writing by Seller and Purchaser. The purchase price, after adjustments are made, shall be paid to Seller in cash, by wire transfer, electronic transfer, certified, treasurer's or bank teller's check, check drawn on the trust or escrow account of a real estate broker licensed in the State of Vermont, or, check drawn on the trust or escrow account of an attorney licensed in the State of Vermont, or any combination of the foregoing. Seller and Purchaser agree that at the Closing, upon request, the brokers named in Section 31 of this Contract shall be provided with a copy of the Settlement Statement/HUD-1 signed by Seller and Purchaser. In the event Seller requests funds by wire transfer or by certified, treasurer's or bank teller's check, Seller shall provide notice thereof to the Attorney or Settlement Agent closing the transaction within a reasonable time prior to the date scheduled for Closing. All fees or charges incurred to enable funds to be paid to Seller by

wire transfer, certified, treasurer's or bank teller's check shall be paid for at Closing by Seller. **Unless otherwise agreed to in writing, or as directed by the Attorney or Settlement Agent closing the transaction, all Contract Deposit(s) held by Escrow Agent shall be paid directly to Seller at Closing and credited toward the total proceeds to be paid to Seller at Closing. . In the event the Attorney or Settlement Agent closing the transaction requests Escrow Agent to deliver the Contract Deposit prior to the date set for Closing, Seller and Purchaser hereby authorize Escrow Agent to do so, provided the Contract Deposit funds are made payable to the closing Attorney or Settlement Agent's trust or escrow account and provided further Escrow Agent reasonably believes the Closing shall occur as scheduled.**

When you write out a deposit check it typically is in the form of a personal check, highly acceptable because the funds will typically be cleared by your bank within 7 days. But when it comes time to close, you need to bring the equivalent of cash, most often a cashier's/bank check. Wiring of funds is fine, you just need to do it about a week prior so the wire arrives on time. We recently had a buyer show up at closing with the intention to wire funds; he pulled out his cell phone and began to proceed with wiring instructions right at the closing table. Sorry, funds still don't clear that fast, in fact occupancy and closing happened in this case days later.

16. **Deed:** Unless otherwise agreed to in writing, Seller shall deliver to Purchaser at Closing a Vermont Warranty Deed, prepared and paid for by Seller, conveying marketable title to the Property as defined by Vermont law.

Most typically you will get a Warranty Deed, unless it is a foreclosure or something along those lines.

17. **Property Transfer Tax/Land Gains Tax/Act 250 Disclosure Statement:** Purchaser shall pay any Vermont Property Transfer Tax due on account of the sale of the Property. If any Ver-

mont Land Gains Tax is due as a result of the sale of the Property, the Seller shall pay such tax as may be due, except as otherwise provided by law or by addendum to this Contract. At or prior to closing, Seller shall provide Purchaser with satisfactory proof either that there is no such tax due or that the tax has been paid in full, or shall provide a certificate from the Vermont Department of Taxes specifying the amount of any tax that may be due as a result of the sale. In the event Seller is required to provide Purchaser with an Act 250 Disclosure Statement and fails to provide such a statement or provides the statement in an untimely manner, Purchaser's closing on this transaction and acceptance of Seller's deed shall constitute a waiver and release of Purchaser's right to declare this Contract unenforceable, to rescind this transaction or to pursue Seller for damages arising out of the failure to provide an Act 250 Disclosure Statement.

This paragraph deals with various taxes, as the buyer you should be aware of the property transfer tax (some states have doc stamps that both the buyer and seller may need to pay). Currently in Vermont the buyer pays the transfer tax. As of this writing the tax is $500 for the first $100,000 and then 1 ¼% thereafter. If you are buying the property as an investment property, the entire amount is taxed at 1 ¼%.

18. **Income Tax Withholding Requirements if Seller is a Non-resident of Vermont and/or Subject to Tax Under the U.S. Foreign Investment in Real Property Tax Act:** If Seller is a nonresident of Vermont, unless a withholding certificate is issued by the Vermont Commissioner of Taxes in advance of the closing, Purchaser shall withhold 2.5 percent of the total purchase price and file a Withholding Tax Return with the Vermont Department of Taxes. In addition, if the sale of the Property subjects Seller to the payment of federal tax under the Foreign Investment in Real Property Tax Act (FIRP-TA), unless a withholding certificate is issued by the Internal Revenue Service, Purchaser shall withhold 10 percent of the

total purchase price and file a Withholding Tax Return with the Internal Revenue Service. If Purchaser fails to withhold such taxes when required to do so, Purchaser may be liable to the respective taxing authorities for the amount of such tax. Purchaser shall have the right to reasonably request evidence that Seller is exempt from payment of either tax in the form of a certificate of residence or non-foreign status. In the event Purchaser is determined to be liable for the payment of either tax, Seller shall indemnify and hold Purchaser harmless from all such liability together with any interest, penalties and reasonable expenses, including attorneys' fees, incurred by Purchaser.

If the seller is moving out of state, they may be subject to having 2 ½% withheld from the State of Vermont, and if they are moving out of the country, the feds could take 10%.

19. **Purchaser's Examination of Title:** Purchaser, at his or her sole cost and expense, shall cause the title to the Property to be examined and shall notify Seller in writing, prior to the date set for Closing, of the existence of any encumbrances or defects which are not accepted in this Contract which render title unmarketable as defined by Vermont law. In such event, Seller shall have thirty (30) calendar days from the time Seller receives such notice to remove the specified encumbrances or defects. Promptly following receipt of such notice, Seller shall exercise reasonable efforts and diligence to remove or cure the specified encumbrances or defects. If, at the expiration of thirty (30) calendar days from the receipt of such notice, or on the date set for Closing, whichever is later, Seller is unable to convey marketable title free and clear of such encumbrances or defects, Purchaser may terminate this Contract, and, if so, shall receive all Contract Deposit(s) and, in addition, may pursue all legal and equitable remedies provided by law, including any damages incurred after the thirty day (30) period referred to above.

The most important job your attorney has is to do a thorough title search. They will check the public records to find the history of the property making certain that the seller has full legal rights to convey the property. You'd be surprised how often an attorney will unearth a former mortgage that is not discharged properly. Ultimately, the attorney will work with the seller's attorney to clear up any discovered issues, but if they can't correct them within 30 days you can choose to terminate the contract.

20. **Default:** If Purchaser fails to close as provided herein, or is otherwise in default, Seller may terminate this Contract by written notice to Purchaser, receive all Contract Deposit(s) as liquidated damages, and, in addition, may pursue all legal and equitable remedies provided by law. If Seller fails to close, or is otherwise in default, Purchaser may terminate this Contract by written notice to Seller, shall receive all Contract Deposit(s) and, in addition, may, subject to the provisions of Section 19 relating to the 30 day cure period for title encumbrances or defects, pursue all legal and equitable remedies provided by law. In the event legal action is instituted arising out of a breach of this Contract, the substantially prevailing party shall be entitled to reasonable attorney's fees and court costs.

I like to call this the McDonalds clause, heck if you spill obviously hot coffee on your lap, a sue-happy person can sue for damages. It is extremely rare that buyers and sellers will sue each other, but it's always a possibility. The prevailing party could win damages along with court and attorney fees.

21. **Contract Deposits:** At Closing and transfer of title, Escrow Agent shall disburse all Contract Deposit(s). In the event Purchaser terminates this Contract under the specific provisions hereof entitling Purchaser to terminate, upon written demand, Escrow Agent shall refund all Contract Deposit(s) to Purchaser in accordance with laws and regulations applicable to Escrow Agent. In the event either Seller or Purchaser does not per-

form and fails to close on the terms specified herein, this shall constitute a default. In the event of a default undisputed by Seller and Purchaser, upon written demand, Escrow Agent shall pay all Contract Deposit(s) to the non-defaulting party in accordance with laws and regulations applicable to Escrow Agent. In such case, Seller and Purchaser agree to execute and deliver to Escrow Agent an Authorization for Delivery of All Contract Deposit(s) to the party entitled to such Deposit(s). In the event Seller or Purchaser provides written notice to the other party of a claimed default and demands delivery of all Contract Deposit(s) on account of such claimed default, if the party to whom such notice is sent disagrees, that party shall provide notice to the party demanding all Contract Deposit(s) and to the Escrow Agent named in Section 5 of this Contract that it demands to mediate the dispute under Section 24 of this Contract. **If such demand to mediate is not sent within twenty-one (21) calendar days from the date written notice of a claimed default was sent, the failure to send such demand to mediate shall constitute authorization and permission under this Contract for Escrow Agent to pay all Contract Deposit(s) to the party claiming default and demanding the Contact Deposit(s) without further notice, documentation or authorization from either Seller or Purchaser.** Payment of all Contract Deposit(s) by the Escrow Agent under such circumstances shall constitute the final resolution and disposition of all Contract Deposit(s). Seller and Purchaser acknowledge and agree that resolution of all Contract Deposit(s) in this manner fully and completely satisfies all laws, regulations and obligations applicable to Escrow Agent and agree to release, discharge, hold harmless and indemnify Escrow Agent acting in good faith pursuant to this section.

In the event mediation is demanded and the dispute over all Contract Deposit(s) is resolved by mediation, Seller and Purchaser agree to instruct Escrow Agent, in writing, as to the disposition and payment of all Contract Deposit(s). In the event the dispute over all Contract Deposit(s) is not resolved by mediation, Escrow Agent shall continue to hold all Contract Deposit(s) in escrow or may, at any time, pay all Contract Deposit(s) into court for the purpose of determining the rights of the parties to all Contract Deposit(s). All costs and expenses of any such action, including attorney's fees incurred by Escrow Agent, shall be borne jointly and severally by Seller and Purchaser irrespective of the amount of all Contract Deposit(s) and irrespective of which party ultimately prevails in the dispute. In the event of a dispute concerning default or payment of all Contract Deposit(s) by Escrow Agent, Escrow Agent shall not be personally liable to either party except for bad faith or gross neglect. In the event a claim other than for bad faith or gross neglect is asserted against Escrow Agent, the parties shall jointly and severally indemnify and hold Escrow Agent harmless from all loss or expense of any nature, including attorney's fees, arising out of the holding of all Contract Deposit(s) irrespective of the amount of all Contract Deposit(s).

Another tough one, very important to pay attention to timelines and make sure these are all done in writing with proper written notice to the seller. As escrow agents, Realtors or Attorneys holding the deposit cannot loosely release the deposit to either party without just cause. Pay special attention to the 21 days specified as to the demand on the deposit. Deposits are not to be made lightly; this is a legal and binding contract. While your agent can help you walk through a disputed deposit, getting your attorney involved may help resolve the matter more quickly.

22. **Terms and Conditions of Interest on Contract Deposit(s):** If interest on all Contract Deposit(s) is reasonably expected to accrue less than One Hundred Dollars ($100.00), all Contract Deposit(s) must be deposited in Escrow Agent's pooled inter-

est bearing real estate trust (IORTA) account as required by Vermont law. The interest accrued on all Contract Deposit(s) will be remitted to the Vermont Housing Finance Agency (VHFA) for the benefit of affordable housing programs in Vermont. Seller and Purchaser acknowledge that this remittance is mandatory under Vermont's Interest on Real Estate Trust Accounts law. If all Contract Deposit(s) is/are reasonably expected to accrue more than One Hundred Dollars ($100.00) in interest, it will be deposited in an individual interest bearing account with a financial institution doing business in Vermont unless Seller and Purchaser authorize Escrow Agent to deposit the Contract Deposit(s) in the Escrow Agent's IORTA account. Any individual interest-bearing account shall obtain a reasonable prevailing rate of interest, provided, Escrow Agent shall have no obligation to obtain the highest available rate of interest. The Purchaser's social security or other federal identification number shall be used to open any individual interest bearing account and to fulfill all reporting responsibilities to governmental authorities concerning such account.

Unless otherwise agreed in writing, Seller and Purchaser agree that all Contract Deposit(s) shall be deposited in Escrow Agent's IORTA account even if interest thereon is expected to earn more than One Hundred Dollars ($100.00)

Bottom line is that placing deposits into an interest bearing account is rarely warranted because per Vermont law all interest shall be given to the Vermont Housing Finance agency to assist in their first time buyer programs. With todays' interest rates, it would need to be a massive deposit to ever exceed the $100 amount.

23.   **Mediation of Disputes:** In the event of any dispute or claim arising out of or relating to this Contract, to the Property, or to the services provided to Seller or Purchaser by any real estate agent who brought about this Contract, it is agreed that such

41

dispute or claim shall be submitted to mediation prior to the initiation of any lawsuit. The party seeking to mediate such dispute or claim shall provide notice to the other party and/or to the real estate agent(s) with whom mediation is sought and thereafter the parties and/or real estate broker(s) with whom mediation is sought shall reasonably cooperate and agree on the selection of a mediator. A party or real estate broker not involved in the dispute or claim shall not be required to participate in the mediation. The real estate agent(s) who brought about this Contract can be of assistance in providing information as to sources for obtaining the services of a mediator. Unless otherwise agreed to in writing, the parties and any real estate agent(s) involved in the mediation shall share the mediator's fee equally. Seller, Purchaser and the real estate agent(s) who brought about this Contract acknowledge and understand that, although utilizing mediation in an effort to resolve any dispute or claim is mandatory under this Contract, the function of the mediator is to assist the parties involved in the mediation in resolving such dispute or claim and not to make a binding determination or decision concerning the dispute or claim. This provision shall be in addition to, and not in replacement of, any mediation or alternative dispute resolution system required by an order or rule of court in the event the dispute results in a lawsuit. *In the event a lawsuit is initiated without first resorting to mediation as required by this Section, any party or real estate agent named in Section 31 of this Contract, shall be entitled to reimbursement of the reasonable cost of attorney's fees or other expenses arising out of such lawsuit until the mediation required by this Section occurs.*

Mediation is a process to try to solve a dispute before actually taking the step of going to court. Perhaps I am old fashioned, but it seems to me both parties are better off if they work through mediation versus going to court.

24. **Fixtures and Personal Property:** Insofar as any of the following items are now located on and belong to the Property, they shall be deemed to be fixtures and are included in this sale; heating, lighting and plumbing fixtures; storm windows and doors; screens and screen doors; curtain rods, window shades and blinds; shrubbery and trees; wall-to-wall carpeting, television antennae and satellite dish. **NO PERSONAL PROPERTY, INCLUDING TELEVISION(S) AND TELEVISION MOUNTING BRACKET(S), IS INCLUDED IN THIS SALE UNLESS EXPRESSLY IDENTIFIED AND DESCRIBED IN THIS CONTRACT OR IN ANY SCHEDULE ATTACHED HERETO.** Any personal property transferred under this Contract is sold "As Is" with no warranties of any kind, express or implied, other than the warranty of title.

While personal property such as stove and refrigerator will appear in the General Addendum, this paragraph stipulates what defines a fixture. The latest addition is the television brackets, they are not included unless addressed elsewhere.

25. **Risk of Loss/Insurance:** During the period between the date of this Contract and the transfer of title, risk of loss shall be on Seller. Seller shall continue to carry such fire and extended coverage insurance as is presently maintained on the buildings and improvements located on the Property. In the event any of the buildings or improvements are destroyed or damaged and are not restored to their present condition by the date set for closing, Purchaser may either accept title to the Property and receive the benefit of all insurance monies recovered on account of such damage or may terminate this Contract and be entitled to the return of all Contract Deposit(s) as Purchaser's sole remedy.

If the home you are buying has damage from a fire or perhaps a hurricane you have the option of terminating or agreeing to the repairs or insurance settlement. Stranger things have happened, especially during Hurricane Irene.

26. **Closing Adjustments:**

    A.   Real property taxes, municipal taxes, fees and assessments, condominium assessments, rents, utilities or similar items shall be apportioned and prorated at Closing between Seller and Purchaser with Seller being responsible for closing adjustments and expenses until the day before Closing and Buyer being responsible for those expenses on and after the day of Closing.

    B.   Should any tax, charge or assessment be undetermined on the date of Closing, the last determined tax charge or rate shall be used for purposes of apportionment and proration.

    C.   Any payment under the Vermont Statewide Education Property Tax which reduces the real estate property tax on the Property, either for the current tax year or thereafter, shall be allocated and paid to Seller at Closing unless the Seller and Purchaser otherwise agree in writing. ***Purchaser is advised that the payment to be made to the Seller at Closing on account of any applicable Statewide Education Property Tax may require Purchaser to have available funds at Closing that might significantly exceed funds for closing adjustments that would otherwise be required.***

    D.   Purchaser shall reimburse Seller at Closing for fuel at the Property at the current rate charged by the Seller's fuel supplier at the time of Closing.

    E.   The net amount of the above adjustments shall be added to or deducted from the amount due to or owed by Seller at Closing.

Essentially, you pay for your time of ownership, and the seller pays for the time they live there, simple enough. The only odd one here is the proration of the Statewide Education Property Tax, this could be quite substantial especially if the seller's income s on the low side. We have seen shocked buyers having to cough up thousands unexpectedly. Not always an easy task, not all is lost though, you would receive at least the remaining balance of tax benefits derived from the seller's low income until the conclusion of the tax year.

27. **Effect:** This Contract is for the benefit of and is binding upon Seller and Purchaser, and their respective heirs, successors, administrators, executors and assigns. This Contract, together with any written and signed addenda thereto, contains the entire agreement by and between Seller and Purchaser and supersedes any and all prior agreements, written or oral. This Contract shall be governed by the laws of the State of Vermont.

What can I say, we need all parties to stay healthy and alive through closing and hopefully for years beyond, otherwise the estate would be equally bound to the contract.

28. **Modification and Amendment:** No change, modification, amendment, addition or deletion affecting this Contract shall be effective unless in writing and signed by Seller and Purchaser.

If either party wishes to modify this contract, that can happen, just need both parties to agree in writing.

29. **Notice:** All notices required to be given under this Contract shall be deemed given when delivered by electronic means that comply with Federal and Vermont electronic signature laws. In addition, any required notice may be delivered by hand, courier or delivery service, or when deposited in the U.S. Mail, certified, registered or express mail, return receipt requested, postage prepaid and properly addressed to Seller or

Purchaser at the respective address for each set forth in this Contract. Any required notice may also be sent by facsimile transmission (fax) of a signed document or by a scanned or digital, signed document or image sent by electronic means. **Other means of electronic transmission, including e-mails without a scanned or digital, signed documents or image attached to such electronic transmission are not adequate to create a Contract or to modify, amend, change or provide any notice required under this Contract.** In the event notices are delivered by hand, courier or delivery service or sent by regular U.S. Mail, such notices shall be effective upon receipt. **Any notice required to be given under this Contract shall be effective only if provided <u>directly</u> to Seller, Purchaser or an attorney representing Seller or Purchaser in the transaction in the manner required by this section. Any notice required to be given under this Contract shall be ineffective if provided <u>only</u> to the real estate agent(s) identified in Section 31 of this Contract.**

Clearly a phone call is not sufficient for a legal notice, and text and emails are not currently going to cut it either. Electronic signatures are acceptable because they can ultimately be traced to the intending party (some lenders are still not allowing electronic signatures). The old fashioned snail mail or couriers such as Fed/Ex and UPS are acceptable means, even hand deliver. My suggestion is that if it matters to you, send the notice direct to the seller yourself is as many ways possible. NO, telling your real estate agent is not acceptable as a means of notice, they can assist you, but the responsibility of notice is fully yours.

30. **Creation of Binding Contract.** No binding Contract shall be created or deemed to exist between Seller and Purchaser unless all terms and conditions of any offer(s) and/or counteroffer(s) (including any addenda) are agreed to in writing, **signed** (or

initialed) by **both** Seller and Purchaser and **notification** thereof provided to the other party at the mailing address(es) including any email address(es) set forth on Page 1 of this Contract in the manner required by Section 29 not later than

_____

_____, 20_____ by ☐ _ A.M./☐ P.M. EST/EDT. Either party has the right to withdraw any offer made prior to acceptance and notification of acceptance by the other party.

In the event a binding Contract is not made by the above date and time, neither party shall have any obligations to the other party. Oral communication of any offer or oral notification of acceptance of any offer is not sufficient to create a legally binding Contract.

This one can get everyone in big trouble, it sets out deadlines of acceptance. A contract is not legally binding until all parties have initialed every minor detail. If another offer comes in that the seller likes more, unless your offer is fully executed, they can accept the new offer even if they had communicated their good intentions. Deadlines matter, time really is of the essence.

31.   **Efforts of Agent(s):** Seller and Purchaser agree that _____ _____ as listing agency representing

Seller and _____

_____

☐ as broker's agent acting as agent of listing agency, ☐ as buyer's agent representing Purchaser, (check only one)

Simply names of the real estate companies and whom they represent in the sale.

32.   **Calendar Days/Counterparts:** Whenever this Contract or an addendum or amendment thereto refers to a day or days,

it shall be deemed to be calendar days. This Contract may be executed in two or more counterparts, each of which shall be deemed an original but all of which shall constitute one and the same Contract.

Calendar days is what is meant when not otherwise specified to be business days.

33. **Time is of the Essence.** Time is of the essence with respect to all obligations and undertakings of Seller and Purchaser under this Agreement <u>including the times for providing all notices required to be given.</u> Failure to act within the time period required shall constitute a breach of this Contract.

As I previously stated, time does matter.

34. **Purchaser's Acknowledgment of Disclosures.** Purchaser acknowledges receipt of the following documents prior to making this offer:

   ☐ Vermont Real Estate Commission Required Consumer Information Disclosure.

   ☐ Vermont Department of Health – Pamphlet – "Testing Drinking Water From Private Water Supplies" (if the Property is served by a private water system)

Last but not least, you are indicating that you have received the Vermont Real Estate Commission Required Consumer Information Disclosure (spells out the difference between Customer and Client, keep in mind that if you have not signed a Buyer Broker Agreement, you need to assume the agent you are working with is not working for your best interest). In addition, if you are buying a home with a well, you should have been given the Vermont Department of Health pamphlet "Testing Drinking Water From Private Water Supplies".

DEAL'S DONE, LET THE GAMES BEGIN

Now, that was easy—or so you thought. I said earlier that the road ahead has many turns, so what's ahead? Finance application, building inspection, renegotiating due to inspection, radon mitigation, appraisal, walkthrough, and finally the closing.

So how do you eat an elephant? One bite at a time. Same holds true for buying a home. The good news is, you are not alone. Your team, which now consists of a great Realtor, a helpful lender, and a protective attorney, will be there to guide you every step of the way. In my opinion, at this stage, it is really having a good Realtor's closing coordinator that makes it all seamless. Our closing coordinator is Rebecca, and she walks on water in our clients' eyes. She makes sure everyone adheres to the contract: buyer, seller, and, yes, me—the Realtor.

We have created "What's Next" reports for our buyers, regarding inspections, appraisals, walkthroughs, and closing. Below is a piece of our "What's Next" regarding inspections.

Inspection is next – This is one of the biggest hurdles in any sale; in fact, more deals die because of the inspection than from any other cause.

1) Keep in mind that the purpose of the building inspection is to unearth any unknowns about the home, especially safety items. The inspector will generate a report that may include dozens of recommendations, all of it sounds dire. Truth be told almost any item can be solved. This is not a time to re-negotiate on items we already know about when we made the offer, it truly is about unknowns. Most often buyers whittle down the list of dozens to something closer to 3-5 items. You have to decide how fussy you wish to be.

2) Inspections can take up to 3 hours, for a condo usually closer to 1.5 hours. In addition to yourself and the inspector attending, you can have a family member or friend attend. Different real estate companies have established policies either allowing for their Realtors

If you'd like to see the full report, as well as others, scan the QR code or go to the website below.

www.condoguy.com/whatsnext

Every state has different contract laws and different state agencies that are involved in the homebuying process. The list of inspections varies according to property type and physical location. In Florida it is common to have inspectors for termites and other critters, hurricane preparedness, sinkholes, and a slew of other potential disasters.

In Vermont it's too dammed cold for termites; hence, no need for that inspection. Termites are marching north, however; one day termite inspections may be required here as well.

As I previously mentioned, within the contract there are several deadlines that must be adhered to or you risk losing your deposit money. Yes, this is serious stuff. That's why you need to be aware of all the critical dates. A good closing coordinator will create and share a critical date summary like the one below. Tape it to your refrigerator and listen to your version of Rebecca. Most of our buyers are great about getting the required paperwork back to us in time; with others, we need to crack the whip. Having fun yet?

PENDING SALE - CRITICAL DATES PURSUANT TO CONTRACT

123 Main Street, Burlington VT

(Property Address)

Buyer(s)   Joe Buyer   Seller(s)   Robert Seller

Effective Date of Contract   3/27/2013

			Date to be Completed
Initial Deposit of	$ 2,000 Due Date		4/3/2013
Additional Deposit	$ n/a Due Date		n/a
Deadline for Loan Application	5 (Days from Effective Date)		4/2/2013
Deadline for Deliver of Condo Documents			4/10/2013
Structure Inspection Done	7 Days from Effective Date		4/5/2013
Structure Inspection Notify Seller	3 Days from Inspection		4/8/2013
Radon Test Done	15 Days from Effective Date		4/17/2013
SPIR done	3 Days from Effective Date		3/30/2013
Fire Safety Inspection Due			5/1/2013
Appraisal Due Date			5/8/2013
Financing Deadline (per paragraph 6 of the contract)			5/8/2013

Special Clauses/Congingencies:

0

Closing Date   5/15/2013

Don't forget to call us to schedule use of the Free Moving Truck!

Prepared on   3/37/2013   by Rebecca James

These are all initial deadlines as written in the contract. Dates may changed based on addendums or negotiations in the future.

www.CondoGuy.com
802-655-9100

Rebecca James

Scan the QR code, or visit www.condoguy.com/closingcoordinator to find out more about how a closing coordinator like Rebecca smooths out the sale and keeps us all on track.

BACK TO THE BANKER

I know; you already met with the banker once to get the preapproval; isn't that enough? Sorry, most lenders spend about fifteen minutes to create a preapproval letter. Mostly it's based on your word and, perhaps, your credit score. It's a decent snapshot, but it's hardly thorough enough for the bank to feel comfortable loaning you hundreds of thousands of dollars. This time, they mean business; and by the time you are done, they will be in touch with your employers, will have reviewed your bank statements, potentially looked at your tax returns, reviewed your divorce decree, and look into anything else that helps them decide if you are creditworthy. A trip to a proctologist might seem less intrusive. But no stone will be left unturned now, especially since the 2008 financial meltdown. And guess what? A day or so before the scheduled closing, they are likely to re-verify much of the same info.

This is a great time to share the "I will not" list with you. Violate any of these, and there is a decent chance your home purchase will be thrown into jeopardy.

I WILL NOT...

- I will not quit my job or change jobs.
- I will not close any bank accounts.
- I will not transfer large sums of money without talking to my lender first.
- I will not apply for new credit or increase credit lines.
- I will not make any big purchases on my credit cards (e.g., new furniture, etc.).
- I will not get any other loans, such as a loan for a new car.

TORN BETWEEN A SINGLE-FAMILY HOME AND A CONDO

Most often, when we meet with buyers, they have already decided between buying a single-family home or a condo. Many remain torn between the two, however, and it doesn't always come down to the cost—it comes down to the buyer's lifestyle. So let's weigh some of the advantages and disadvantages of each; hopefully, this will lead to a great decision supported by a touch of reason. Recently I read the book *Sway*, by Ori Brafman, and I was forced to acknowledge how often I (and most human beings) make irrational decisions. My hope is that if you're able to drill down not only on your list of needs and wants, but also on which style of home makes the most sense for you at this time, you'll be making a rational decision, rather than being swayed by an emotional pull.

A couple of years ago, a good friend of mine decided, on a whim, to buy a bigger home just down the street from her last home. Keep in mind that she was a single mom of one wonderful girl. Financially, she was a steady wage earner; in fact, she was at the top of her field. Yet, like so many Americans, she always found a way to spend to the limits of her capabilities. (After all, who doesn't like to shop?) Her home at the time was 2,400 square feet, much of which was underutilized; and yet she felt the need to get a bigger home with more cleaning requirements and still higher costs. Little consideration was made for the fact that her daughter would be off to college the next year, and the household would shrink down to one. Not to mention she had a rather full plate: lots of friends, elderly family members to care for and to visit, a seventy-hour work week, running, a personal exercise trainer, and skiing. Oh, I forgot to mention travel; although she has a ways to go to catch up with the likes of Hillary Clinton, she has traveled to virtually every corner of the globe.

The big home became a reality, and soon thereafter, reality set in. Yes, she loved the larger yard, and it was great to dream of the days of entertaining. As it turned out, life was way too busy to entertain in her beautiful new home, and the upkeep added even more stress to an already stressed life filled with way too many to-dos.

Fast forward to today—and yes, I do mean today, for as I type, she is moving once again. This time, she has chosen a lovely townhouse condo with plenty of space to spread her wings. But this time she doesn't have to think about shoveling the snow, mowing the lawn this summer, or raking the leaves next fall. She also doesn't have to worry about major repair costs that always fall at the worst of times; roofs, after all, are very expensive. Some things will take getting used to, like living by the rules of the condo association, having little say in what outside projects get done, and having limited control over the monthly association fees. It's a balancing act, and only you know what's best based on who you are.

Thus, when it comes time to decide what type of housing you really should be focusing on, it makes tons of sense to face your personal reality dead on. Keeping in mind that throughout life, things change, I, for one, have gone from the duplex condo to a single-family home, and then back to a condo, to a single-family, to a condo, to a duplex, back to a condo, followed by another condo, and now I live in a single-family home. By now you may think I am one confused individual (ever so true). But much of these changes represented different phases in my life: married, divorced, in a relationship, job transfers, whole new careers, financial limits, three different cities, and a host of other life changes.

Life keeps on changing. Some people don't move but every twenty to thirty years. The average American under forty is likely to move within the next three to five years; many will move more than once. What phase of life are you in? Have you given consideration to what lies ahead for you? Change is inevitable, but it sure would be nice to acknowledge where you are on this path through life. Let's chat about the nuances of both a single-family home and a condo.

SINGLE-FAMILY…IT ALL SOUNDS SO WHOLESOME

What's there to like about a single-family home? Lots. First off, you don't have to get anyone's permission to make changes to the home, other than the local zoning authority. You want to paint your home pink? Go for it. Thinking it's time to add a screened-in porch? No one will stop you. Feeling like planting an organic garden that will be the envy of your friends? Plant away. With freedom comes some challenges. Who's got the time to paint the house pink or can afford the cost of hiring the pros? You might not get bitten by mosquitoes when sitting outside on your new porch, but is it really going to add value, or are you flushing ten thousand dollars down the drain? About that garden, how much time can you devote to pulling weeds? When you choose to own a single-family home, all of the burdens fall onto your shoulders. So if you have septic problems, leaky roofs, and cracked driveways, you are responsible.

So when you are writing an offer, be certain you have thoroughly reviewed the sellers' property information report (SPIR); make sure you know the status of any septic system, and have a pro determine the likely timeframe to replace the roof. And if you live in the country, with some acreage, make sure you know the boundaries. If you have time to walk slowly though the neighborhood, I am willing to bet some nosey neighbors can give you some insight on the property you are considering. Your attorney will be checking on title issues, but you need to make sure you know how solid the home is. There aren't any perfect homes, but it makes sense to unearth any likely large expenditures. Condos can have many of the same issues, but typically the condominium management company or association has planned for any upcoming capital expenditures such as siding and roofs.

CONDOS ARE A DIFFERENT BEAST

I have often been asked how I chose to become the Condo Guy. Truth be known, the name more or less chose me. My first involvement to condominiums was way back in the '70s when my brother hired me to tar the foundation of one of Vermont's first condo projects. Later, I graduated to staining all the woodwork within a twelve-unit condo project in Colchester, Vermont. The very first time I handled the initial sales of a condo project, it was a gentrification project on Lakeview Terrace. I was very proud to be the go-to guy for this sweet cluster of condos—partly because it was the first time a developer trusted me with such a large development, but also because it was on the street I grew up on in the Old North End of Burlington. Through the years I have been privileged to handle the initial sales of countless condo projects for developers throughout Vermont. Milot Development hired me for Overlook, the Landings, Harborwatch, Eastcreek, and others; Homestead Design hired me to handle their seventy units at Southwind by the Lake; Farwater hired me for Cedar Bluff; Snyder hired me for Highland Village; Farrell hired me for Eastwood Commons I and II; Champlain Housing Trust hired me for City's Edge...the list goes on and on. But the name "the Condo Guy" came to me while I was walking down the hall at RE/MAX North Professionals. My wonderful colleague Jan Lawson said, "Hey, condo guy," and the rest is history. So, although to this day I have still sold more single-family homes than 90 percent of the Realtors in the area, much of my focus has been on condos. Thus, without sounding too bold, I can say I know a thing or two about condominium ownership.

Within the general heading of condominiums, or condos, there are a variety of styles and types of ownerships. Often, from the outside, it is very difficult to tell whether it is a true condominium, a co-op, or perhaps what's called a PUD (Planned Unit Development). Most states do not have co-ops, but New York, Florida, California, and a few others throughout the United States do. Of all the co-ops in the country, half are in New York City. Indeed, there are close to 1.2 million co-ops in the United States, but for this book, I will be focusing on condominium ownership. At the back of the book, you will find my definitions of the various styles of home ownership, as well as all the peculiar language of the entire buying process.

Condos come in many different styles and are in different types of buildings. In my state they include flats, garden units, townhouses, and carriage homes. Most have one thing in common: collectively, the homeowners share in common expenses and must abide by a slew of governing documents. These documents can be fifty to one hundred pages long. Don't be overwhelmed; most are related to how the condo association was initially formed and how the voting occurs. The biggest portion of the condo documents is the bylaws and declaration; these define the ownership component, how officers are elected, and how meetings are conducted. The ones you need to pay close attention to are the operating budget, financial statement, resale certificate/estoppel certificate, annual general meeting minutes, board meeting minutes, and the rules and regulations.

If you're not buying a condo, fast forward to the next section. This may just bore the heck out of you. Dry material, granted—but ever so important to know. I have loved my condo ownership over the years, but I have always known just what I was getting into before signing on the dotted line. Allow me to go into some depth on each of the documents mentioned above.

Operating Budget—The operating budget (OB) for the current fiscal year sets out what the anticipated expenses are; typically, they include at least the following but vary from one association to the other: landscaping, rubbish removal, snow removal, master insurance, building maintenance, pool care, management fees, legal/accounting fees, and reserves. Critically, make sure the association has a specific line item of at least 10 percent for reserves; otherwise, homeowners are likely to face challenges with financing, thus impacting salability.

Financial Statements—Not all associations keep financial statements, as scary as that sounds. The financial statement gives you a summary of where the association stands financially. One of the most important items you can find here is the amount they have in a reserve fund. This will always appear in the resale certificate/estoppel certificate as well. If the reserves are too low, you will likely face a special assessment in the near future which leads us to the minutes from meetings.

Annual Meeting and Board Meeting Minutes—At each meeting, someone is in charge of taking notes and sending those notes to all the owners; these notes are what are called *minutes*. You need to become an expert at reading between the lines; if there have been prior discussions of some issues that clearly will need addressing or some investments down the road, you will find them buried in the minutes.

Resale Certificate/Estoppel Certificate—Essentially, these two items are the same thing; they just have different names in different states. I believe that this may be the most important piece of paper provided by the condominium association. They vary in length, but here you will get a one- to two-page snapshot on how the association is managing its affairs and will let you know specifically whether the condo you are buying has any delinquencies at this time.

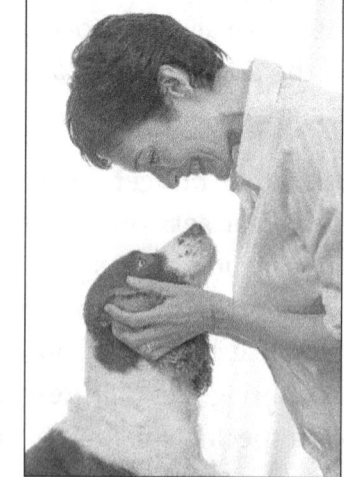

Rules and Regulations—If you don't read these, you have no one to blame when the association comes by to enforce a rule you have unknowingly violated. Yes, they can make Fido move if dogs are not allowed. The association most likely has some form of rental restrictions, a pet rule, rules pertaining to grilling, how many cars are allowed on the premises, and so on. Again, let your agent know at the outset what rules you can't live with; there's no point in falling in love with a condo that doesn't allow your family's pet.

By now you might be wondering, "How can I get these documents, and from whom?" Because much of the information needs to be up-to-the-minute, you normally do not get these documents until you have come to terms with the seller. By law the seller must get you the stack of documents within a set period of time; in Vermont, it is ten days. Once you have received them, you have five days to review them. Keep in mind that when you placed the offer, it would likely have a clause stating that the purchase is subject to you being satisfied with full review of the condo docs. If you don't like what you discover, you can always terminate the contract and receive your deposit back. Just make sure you give notice in time and do it formally, not just in a phone call or e-mail. I know this all seems daunting, but with proper guidance, it truly can be seamless and, yes, even fun.

CLOSING DAY, TIME TO MOVE!

So at last you are reaching the finish line, the day you have been waiting for: closing day. It's strange how the western half of the United States functions differently than the eastern half, but closings are vastly different, depending on where you are buying. In the west, the sale is closed in escrow; quite frequently the buyer and seller never even meet. A third party, such as an attorney or title company, makes sure things are handled smoothly. Where I am from, at most closings, it seems like everyone shows up at the closing; it's one big party, with you being the one with a piñata stick. Just days before the closing, your attorney will have conducted a title search, usually back at least forty years to make sure the property doesn't have any undisclosed liens. There's nothing worse than a former owner showing up one day, laying some kind of claim to your beautiful home.

Your attorney will be at your side, guiding you through the stack of legal documents, which can literally be in the dozens. You can bet that most of the documents protect the bank (bottom line: as long as you pay on time, you won't have any problems). Although most of the documents are standard, don't hesitate to ask for explanations of any documents, especially the note, the deed, and the settlement statement. Most often the closings are rather pleasant; some humor might even enter the fray.

Don't forget that when you go to the closing, you need to bring a certified check, usually made payable to the law firm conducting the closing, which is usually your attorney. Also, you need a photo ID.

After about an hour of endless signing of documents, you pass your check over, and the seller passes you the set of keys. You have now become a fellow member of home ownership, so welcome aboard. This is a moment worthy of celebration; you have followed a path that truly leads in a new direction, one where you are in the driver's seat of your destination. You have graduated from renter to owner; you are now paying off your mortgage and not some landlord. Increased tax savings are now in your hands—as are forced savings, as each month, your net worth grows. These past few years have been trying times for the housing market, yet you know that the future bodes well for you and for those who trust in the American dream. It may seem like a stretch for you to consider right now, but this decision, this choice, has laid the foundation for the rest of your life. You have been bold, even in moments of uncertainty, and you have made it to the other side. Rejoice. A new day has begun.

DON'T MAKE THESE MISTAKES!

1. Continue to rent because it's a bit cheaper.

    Actually, right now, in our marketplace, the cost of renting is higher than what homeownership would be at these amazing prices and interest rates. Not to mention the fact that rents go up on average by at least 3 percent per year, so a $1,000 rent today would be $1,344 in ten years. Even more importantly, you'll be missing out on all of the mortgage interest deductions, which will likely save you thousands of dollars.

2. Wait for prices to fall more.

    Guess what? Prices are already starting to rebound. But even if they weren't, there's a good chance interest rates will be climbing, which means the mortgage payment could actually be higher, even if prices were to fall a tad.

3. Wait for rates to go lower.

    They could, but in my thirty-four years of selling real estate, these are the absolute lowest they've ever been. The federal government has put downward pressure on consumer prices to avoid inflation and has artificially driven down interest rates as well. That's all about to end.

4. Can't afford your dream home and decide to wait.

    Your dream home will be constantly evolving. What works today won't work for you in the coming years. Your income will change, and so will your standards. Why not take advantage of this opportunity today to have a stepping stone to your dream home tomorrow?

5. Decide the economy is too scary.

    First, stop watching NBC and CNN and hearing all the doomsday prophets who cover the economic news. They pretend to have a crystal ball, when in fact, they are largely full of hype. Be mindful of the economy, but remember, everything is cyclical, and we are now on course for a new direction.

6. It's a fantastic home, but I need to see more.

    When will enough be enough? If you're clear on what your needs and wants are, and your gut tells you this is "the one," don't wait—you might just lose out.

7. It's priced well, but I want a steal.

    Don't we all? The reality is, if it's priced well, another buyer will also appreciate the value and may just swoop it up, while you continue to "play not to lose" rather than "play to win."

8. Buying direct from a for-sale-by-owner will save me money.

    When it comes to for-sale-by-owners, they aren't going to be priced lower just because they're not listed with an agent. In fact, I have worked with many people who bought a for-sale-by-owner property without consulting a Realtor and paid way over market value for the home.

9. I'm having cold feet and want to back out.

We deal with this all the time—it's called buyer's remorse. Did I look at enough homes? Did I pay too much? Will something else better come on the market? Once you're under contract for a home, stop looking. My suggestion is to breathe and remember why you fell in love with the home in the first place.

10. Backing out because of the radon test.

Radon occurs in nature; virtually every home (and even the outdoors) has some level of radon. The EPA has set some of the toughest standards in the world when it comes to radon. Don't panic if the radon level comes in above the EPA guidelines, a mitigation system can be installed. Frankly, one of the safest homes may just be one where you know what the radon levels are and the seller has installed a mitigation system, reducing the radon to nearly zero.

11. Not thrilled with my real estate agent—yikes, now what?

I think it's important that you make a decision to work with just one real estate agent, because they can show you every property on the market. The way you show commitment is by entering what can be called a buyer broker agreement. Find out if you have the legal right to exit this agreement if it's truly clear that your business relationship isn't working. My team allows termination with 24 hours notice because if the working relationship is strained, there's no point in continuing down a difficult path.

12. I'm going to use my divorce attorney for real estate.

Different attorneys specialize in different areas of the law, and rarely do they cross into fields not related to their practice. When choosing an attorney, pick one that's a real estate attorney, rather than a divorce attorney or litigation attorney. After all, you wouldn't go to your dentist for open heart surgery!

13. Aunt Sally hasn't sold a home in months, but I feel I need to work with her.

    Aunt Sally may be the sweetest lady in the world, but this is one of the biggest decisions you're going to make in your lifetime. Tell Aunt Sally that you value your friendship so much you don't want a real estate transaction gone sour to jeopardize the precious relationship.

14. Save money by not having a building inspection.

    Oh, really? There are a few times when it might not make a lot of sense to have a building inspection, but 95 percent of the time, I think they're worth it. In fact, not only will they save you money in the long run, they'll help educate you on the ins and outs of what it takes to run the home.

15. Bite off more than you can chew.

    Lending practices continue to evolve. Some lenders allow you to stretch beyond your rational comfort level, so pay attention to it. Living with constant financial stress just isn't worth it. Try to get most of your needs and wants satisfied, but not if it makes you ill whenever the bills come in.

DEADLIEST SIN OF ALL: NOT BUYING

SAMPLE FORMS

_____

(Name of Association)

RESALE CERTIFICATE
27A V.S.A. 4-109

_____ (name of association) hereby

sets forth the following information with respect to Unit/Lot /Apartment No. _____ as of the date set forth below.

1.   Right of first refusal or other restraint on free alienability: _____
_____

2.   Periodic common expense assessment is billed ☐ monthly ☐annually ☐other. The periodic common expense assessment for

the current period is $_____. The total unpaid common expenses and special assessments for this

unit/lot/apartment are $_____.

3.   Other fees payable by the Owner of this unit/lot/apartment are $_____.

4.   The amount of reserves for capital expenditures are as follows: _____
_____. The following portions of the reserves

have been designated by the Association for the following specified projects: _____
_____.

5.   There are no unsatisfied judgments against the Association except _____
_____. There are no pending suits in

which the Association is a party except as follows, and the status of those suits is as follows: _____
_____.

6.   The Executive Board of the Association and the Managing Agent of the Association have no knowledge of violations of health

or building codes with respect to the unit/lot/apartment, any limited common elements assigned to it, or any other portion of

the common interest except _____
_____.

7.   ☐ There is no leasehold estate affecting the common interest community, OR

☐ The remaining term of any leasehold estate affecting the common interest community is _____ years, and the provisions

governing any extension or renewal of such lease are as follows: _____
_____.

8.   There are no restrictions in the declaration affecting the amount that may be received by a unit/lot/apartment owner upon sale,

condemnation or casualty loss to the unit/lot/apartment, or the common interest community, or termination of the common

interest community except: _____
_____.

Attached to this Certificate are the following:
a.   Declaration with all amendments (but excluding plats and plans);
b.   Bylaws of the Association in effect;
c.   Rules and regulations of the Association in effect (if any);
d.   Most recent regularly prepared balance sheet and statement of income and expense for the Association (if any);
e.   Current operating budget of the Association.

Date: _____   By: _____
                                                                                        Name of Association

SELLER'S PROPERTY INFORMATION REPORT
TO BE COMPLETED BY SELLER

Seller's Name(s): _____   Date: _____

_____

Property Address: _____

Type of Property: Single Family Residence,   Multi-Family Residence (duplex, triplex, etc,),   Condominium/Townhouse,
Land Only,   Commercial

INTRODUCTION: This Report provides information from the Seller based on Seller's personal knowledge concerning the above Property. Unless otherwise disclosed, Seller does not have any expertise in construction, architecture, engineering, surveying or any other skills that would provide Seller with special knowledge concerning the condition of the Property. Other than having owned the Property, Seller has no greater knowledge about the Property than that which could be obtained by a careful inspection performed by or on behalf of a potential buyer. The real estate agents involved with the sale of this Property do not conduct or perform any inspection of the Property. Unless otherwise disclosed, Seller has not inspected or examined those portions of the Property that are generally inaccessible. **THIS REPORT DOES NOT CONSTITUTE A WARRANTY OF ANY KIND BY THE SELLER OR BY ANY REAL ESTATE AGENT CONCERNING THE CONDITION OF THE PROPERTY. THIS REPORT IS NOT A SUBSTITUTE FOR A PROPERTY INSPECTION. BUYER HAS THE OPPORTUNITY TO REQUEST THAT SELLER AGREE TO A PROPERTY INSPECTION AS PART OF ANY CONTRACT FOR THE SALE OF THE PROPERTY.**

INSTRUCTIONS TO SELLER: (1) Answer ALL questions. (2) Disclose conditions that you know about that affect the Property. (3) Attach additional pages to this Report if additional information is required. (4) Complete this form yourself. (5) If some items do not apply to this Property, write "N/A" (Not Applicable). IF YOU DO NOT KNOW THE FACTS, WRITE "DON'T KNOW." DO NOT GUESS THE ANSWER TO ANY QUESTION.

**THE STATEMENTS IN THIS REPORT ARE MADE BY THE SELLER.
THEY ARE NOT STATEMENTS OR REPRESENTATIONS MADE BY ANY REAL ESTATE AGENT(S).**

1. LAND (SOILS, DRAINAGE, BOUNDARIES AND EASEMENTS)

(a) Has any fill or off-site material been placed on the Property?   YES   NO   DON'T KNOW

(b) Do you know of any sliding, settling, subsidence, earth movement, upheaval or earth
     stability problems that have occurred on the Property or in the immediate neighborhood?   YES   NO   DON'T KNOW

(c) Is the Property located in a federal flood hazard zone or wetlands, public waters or
     conservation zones designated by federal, state or local statute, regulation or ordinance? YES   NO   DON'T KNOW

(d) Do you know of any past or present drainage, high water table, or flood problems
     affecting the Property or adjacent properties?   YES   NO   DON'T KNOW

(e) Is the Property served by a road maintained by the municipality?   YES   NO   DON'T KNOW

(f) Are there public or private landfills or dumps (compacted or otherwise) on the Property
     or on any abutting property?   YES   NO   DON'T KNOW

(g) Are there currently any underground storage tanks, including gasoline, propane and/or
     fuel oil on the Property?   YES   NO   DON'T KNOW

(h) Have there been any underground storage tanks, including gasoline, propane and/or
     fuel oil on the Property in the past?   YES   NO   DON'T KNOW
     If yes, have they been removed?   YES   NO   DON'T KNOW
     When? _____ By whom? _____

(i) Do you know the location of the boundary lines of the Property?   YES   NO   DON'T KNOW

Seller(s) Initials _____ _____ _____ _____

PURCHASE AND SALE CONTRACT
THIS IS A LEGALLY BINDING CONTRACT

Purchaser's Full Name	Mailing Address (Incl. Zip)	Telephone # / Fax # E-mail Address

Seller's Full Name	Mailing Address (Incl. Zip)	Telephone # / Fax # E-mail Address

1. **Purchase and Sale Contract:** This Purchase and Sale Contract (Contract) is made by and between
    _____ (Seller) and
    _____ (Purchaser).
    Purchaser hereby offers and agrees to purchase from Seller and Seller **agrees** to **sell** and **convey** to Purchaser the Property described herein at the price and on the terms and conditions stated in this Contract.

2. **Total Purchase Price:** _____ U.S. Dollars ($_____)

3. **Contract Deposit:** $_____ (US Dollars) as evidenced by   Personal check   Bank check   Cash   Wire transfer
    Additional Contract Deposit of $_____ **(US Dollars) is due within** _____ **calendar days after Seller's acceptance of offer.**
    Unless otherwise agreed to in writing, the pendency or satisfaction of any contingencies or special conditions to this Contract does not suspend, postpone or affect Purchaser's obligation to make any required additional Contract Deposit.

4. **Description of Real Property:** For purposes of this Contract, the Property is described as follows:

    A. Property Address: _____ ; and/or
        _____ Street _____ City/Town
        Seller's Deed is recorded in Volume _____ at Page(s) _____ of the _____ Land Records; and/or
    B. Parcel ID# (from municipal tax records) _____ and/or
    C. SPAN# _____ ; and/or
    D. The Property is further described as:
        _____
        _____
        _____

    NOTE: *Not every Property Description choice is required to be completed in order to form this Contract. The validity and enforceability of this Contract is not affected by the omission of one or more of the above choices, provided at least one choice is filled in.*

    The deed delivered by Seller at Closing will govern the legal description of the real property to be conveyed under this Contract.

5. **Contract Deposit to be Held By:** _____ ("Escrow Agent"). If Purchaser's offer is not accepted, expires, or is revoked or withdrawn prior to acceptance, the Contract Deposit shall be promptly returned. The Contract Deposit shall accrue interest on the terms and conditions provided in Section 23 of this Contract.

GLOSSARY OF REAL ESTATE TERMS

Amortized Loan.

A loan that is completely paid off, interest and principal, by a series of regular payments that are equal or nearly equal over a set term, the most popular being a period of thirty years.

Appraisal.

A comparison report created by an independent third party to establish market value. The appraisal is paid by the purchaser, to the benefit of the lending institution.

Appreciation.

An increase in value of real estate.

ARM (Adjustable Rate Mortgage).

Also known as a variable-rate mortgage, it is a mortgage loan where the interest rate on the note is periodically adjusted, based on an index that reflects the cost to the lender of borrowing on the credit markets.

Closing.

The final settlement of a real estate transaction between a buyer and seller, where you will be signing close to fifty documents and turning over your cash in exchange for the keys. Then you get to move in!

Condominium.

A system of individual fee ownership of units, combined with joint ownership of common areas of the structure and land.

Conventional Mortgage.

A mortgage secured by a loan without government underwriting, such as FHA or VA.

Counteroffer.

A seller's rejection of an offer made by a buyer, accompanied by an agreement to sell the property to the potential buyer on terms differing from the original offer. Often counteroffers are done verbally rather than in writing.

Deed.

A written instrument that, when properly executed and delivered, conveys title. The most common type is a warranty deed.

Deposit.

The initial portion of a down payment made by the purchaser as evidence of good faith, usually between 1and 2 percent of the sale price. It will be credited to the purchaser at closing.

Easement.

The right, privilege, or interest that one party has in the land of another, such as utility easements.

Equity.

The interest or value an owner has in real estate over and above the liens against the real property.

Fannie Mae.

The nickname of the Federal National Mortgage Association (FNMA), a taxpaying corporation created by Congress to support the secondary mortgages insured by FHA or guaranteed by VA, as well as conventional home mortgages.

FHA Loan.

A loan that has been insured by the federal government, guaranteeing its payment in case of default by the owner.

Firm Commitment.

A lender's agreement to make a loan to a specific borrower on a specific property; an FHA or PMI agreement to insure a loan on a specific property, with a designated purchaser.

Freddie Mac.

The nickname for the Federal Home Loan Mortgage Corporation (FHLMC), a federally controlled and operated corporation to support the secondary mortgage market. It purchases and sells residential conventional home mortgages.

Joint Tenancy.

Joint ownership by two or more persons with right of survivorship; all joint tenants own equal interest and have equal rights in the property.

Lien.

An encumbrance on the property, which usually names the property as security for the payment of a debt, discharge, or obligation. Examples: judgments, taxes, mortgages, deeds of trust.

Loan Commitment.

A written promise by a lender to make a loan under certain terms and conditions. These include interest rate, length of the loan, lender fees, annual percentage rate, mortgage and hazard insurance, and other special requirements.

Loan-to-Value Ratio.

The ratio of the mortgage loan principal (amount borrowed) to the property's appraised value (selling price). On a $100,000 home, with a mortgage loan principal of $80,000, the loan-to-value ratio is 80 percent.

Mortgage/Deed of Trust.

An instrument t recognized by law, by which property is pledged as security or collateral for debt without transfer of title or possession, to secure the payment of a debt or obligation to the lender. The title transfers to the lender during the foreclosure process, which occurs in the event that the debtor defaults on the loan obligation to the lender.

Mortgage Insurance Premium (MIP).

The consideration paid by a mortgagor for mortgage insurance, either to FHA or a private mortgage insurance (PMI) company. It is a part of the regular monthly payment.

Mortgagee.

The lender of money or the receiver of the mortgage document.

Mortgagor.

The borrower of money or the giver of the mortgage document.

Note.

Following a loan commitment from the lender, the borrower signs a written promise to repay the loan under stipulated terms. The note establishes personal liability for its repayment.

Origination Fee.

A fee or charge for the work involved in the evaluation, preparation, and submission of a proposed mortgage loan. Origination fees are paid by the borrower to the lender.

Personal Property.

Any property that is not real property. Examples: money, savings accounts, appliances, cars, boats.

Point.

One percent of the loan amount.

Private Mortgage Insurance (PMI).

Insurance written by a private company, protecting the mortgage lender against loss occasioned by a mortgage default.

Purchase Agreement.

An agreement between a buyer and a seller for the purchase of real estate.

RD (Rural Development) Loan.

A loan insured by the federal government, similar to FHA loans; usually used for residential properties in rural areas.

Real Property.

Any land and whatever is a part of it, by nature or artificial annexation.

Special Assessment.

A legal charge against real estate by a public authority to pay the costs of public improvements, such as street lights, sidewalks, street improvements, and so on.

Subdivision.

A parcel of land that has been divided into smaller parts.

Tenancy in Common.

Ownership by two or more persons who hold undivided interest, without the right of survivorship. Interests need not be equal.

Term of Mortgage.

The period during which a mortgage must be paid; the most common is thirty years.

Title Insurance.

An insurance policy that protects the insured (purchaser or lender) against loss arising from defects in title.

Title Search.

A summary or digest of the conveyances, transfers, and any other facts relied on as evidence of title, together with any other elements or records that may affect the marketability of title.

Trust Account.

An account separate, apart, and physically segregated from a broker's won funds, in which the broker is required by law to deposit all funds collected for clients.

VA (Veterans' Administration) Loan.

A loan guaranteed by the Veterans' Administration.

Warranty Deed.

A deed used to convey real property, which contains warranties of title and quiet possession, and the grantor agrees to defend the premises against unlawful claims of third persons.

www.ingramcontent.com/pod-product-compliance
Lightning Source LLC
Chambersburg PA
CBHW071255170526

45165CB00003B/1350